DISCOVER…

**SECRET $ 100 PERDAY
TECHNIQUE HOW TO MAKE
MONEY FROM INTERNET WHILE
YOU ARE SLEEP**

By

W M HIRWANI W HUSSAIN

Copyright © 2014

Introduction

This book explains the exact techniques to start your business from internet with the simple techniques without hassle. The techniques in this eBooks have been used by the top marketers to generate income from the internet.

Feel free to email me if you need further discussion about the techniques. You can contact me through email at:

Contact details:

wmhwh12@gmail.com

LEGAL NOTES

CHAPTER 1.

INTRODUCTION

There are people who have money and people who are rich.

Coco Chanel

You can make $100 in 24 hours on the Internet. There is no magic button. It takes work but you can do it. Earn means you have completed the work and the money is owed to you.

Using some of the companies included in this report as resources, you can receive payment on a weekly or monthly basis. Many times, when working with individuals, the payment will be made immediately upon completion of the work.

You can make a lot of money by writing and self-publishing your own material, if you are willing to write e-books, articles, reports or newsletters that millions of people across the United States, and throughout the world for that matter, desperately want to buy.

Today, more than ever before, is the age of information. Twenty-four hours a day, seven days a week, there continues to be an incredible demand for information throughout the world. There is an astronomical demand for information-packed eBooks, articles, reports and newsletters of almost every imaginable kind. You can start putting a price on information you have no doubt been giving away.

A lot of people have leveraged the global exposure of internet to market their business. There are people who are so successful in their internet marketing business that they earned their first million dollars in their twenties. Unfortunately there are also those who are still struggling to earn their first thousand dollar every month.

By now, almost everyone has heard about working from home. Some people might have actually attempted to do it but they were not quite successful.

Earning money from home is an attractive practice because you are your own boss and control your own schedule. First, however, you need to familiarize yourself with the workings of Internet marketing.

Anyone hoping to benefit from working at home needs to follow certain steps. With a lot of information about Internet marketing floating around, you need to see the truth from the lies and this article helps to point you in the right direction.

One important thing that you need to remember is that making money online comes in many forms. You need to identify which form works for you and then concentrate on it for a long time. When you gain plenty of skill and expertise then you can try out other forms.

Think about the things that you like doing and how they can help you make money. Doing something that you do not like is as good as useless especially since you have many options available.

Let's take a look at how you can actually join the first group with ease:

Sometimes your best investments are the ones you don't make.

Donald Trump

1. Your goal

Not having a target is why a lot of internet marketer fails in internet marketing. Be it $10,000 or $100,000 dollar a month, you got to have it written in your diary.

Your goal is like the finish line of your race. If you fail to have a goal, you will be running an eternal marathon and chasing an invisible dream.

2. Multiple source of income

Let's say you decide to earn $10,000 from your internet marketing business. Please don't trap yourself to earn that kind of money from just one source. Internet marketing is just a category of marketing online and there are a lot of sub-categories under it.

If you are earning $100 from your website a day, why not join affiliate marketing, blogging and email marketing to earn another $100 from each of them? It is a profitable $400 a day and it is easily earnings of $12000 a month.

3. Focus

You might be wondering how you can focus in the internet marketing business if you stretch yourself thin in other projects. There are just too many things to learn in so short a time.

So, this is where time management and outsourcing kick in. A successful internet marketer knows that he has less than 24 hours to work for his business and that is why he needs to follow his schedule to get things done.

He will then outsource smaller tasks to other talents and allowing himself to focus on the big picture of his internet marketing career.

4. Creating value

Now, this is the big picture you need to focus on. Moos of your visitors are not going to spend money on you on their first visit. They are skeptical to you and your offer. Your visitors are going to ask questions like, "Who are you?", "Is your product going to work or are you going to con my money?"

We go to school to learn to work hard for money. I write books and create products that teach people how to have money work hard for them.

Robert Kiyosaki

#1: Make Money Writing

Ghostwriting articles

Make money online writing an article is something that almost everyone would have heard of by now. There are quite a lot of home based businesses today that can provide you a solid side income or can even replace your day job well. Writing online of the ways in which you can earn money today and a lot of people earn their first online income by writing an article for someone else. Whether you have any experience or not does not matter as long as you can write in decent English and can provide interesting and useful articles. If you like to write then you can easily make money by turning your passion into your job.

Money won't create success, the freedom to make it will.

Nelson Mandela

Why Writing Article

a) Articles are needed by thousands of websites

Make money online writing articles are legitimate and it does work. There are thousands of websites and online businesses today that need content and articles for many reasons. Websites need content for their website, short blog posts, sales copy, articles for promoting their website etc. You will find hundreds of jobs posted online for such requirements and if you are good at writing, you can easily make money by writing for different companies on a regular basis. Although it may take some time initially to find work, once you do complete a few projects for different companies, you can build up on your client base and you will continue to get new projects from the same clients. Recommendations from your clients will also bring in more work for you.

b) No experience needed

Although most people think that they would need to be experienced to make money online writing articles, it is not true. Website owners are more interested in someone who can provide them good quality articles and content and they would not really care whether or not you have any experience as long as you can provide them articles that they like. You can earn money even if you are not experienced. There are several people who have never written articles in their life before but they are eager to learn and they keep writing and learning from their mistakes. However, with experience, you will learn how to make your articles better and you will be able to provide your clients articles that are engaging and interesting.

c) A part-time or full-time business

No matter how much time you have on hands, you can work from home and write articles whenever you are free. Article writing can be a part-time or a full-time job for you. Initially you can start part-time and as you learn more and build up on your client base, you can easily make it a full-time business. Make money online writing articles is a genuine and a very effective way of earning a good amount of money online.

Basically, there are two ways of making money from writing articles, one of which is you write for someone else and other one is for yourself. The example of the former are freelancing or technical writing and of the latter are writing articles for your blog, websites or self-publishing a book. Both the paths of making money have their ups and downs.

In the case, when you are writing for someone else the benefit is that you have all the control and you control your working hours. There is no one to whom you have to answer to. These articles that you write for your own blogs or websites bring in the currency flow all the time. The detriment of this strategy is that the flow of currency though constant but is a late bloomer, i.e. it takes time to earn money as you have to start from the scratch.

While in the other situation, where you write for and get paid by someone else, vice-versa of the above hold true. It means the income enters your pocket soon after the work is completed or in the certain period of time. But apart from the shining side, the disadvantage is there's a sturdy contest and the person with high intellect can only withstand.

You have to have some writing talent to ghostwrite articles. You do need to be organized, able to research topics quickly, summarize the main points and write the article in a clear way, with correct spelling and grammar.

The article length can range from 200 words to 1000 words or more. Payment is usually by the word. For beginners, a 500 word article can be sold for about $5.00. An accomplished ghostwriter can charge up to $30 for a 500 word article.

The client gives you the topic and any key words that must be included in the article. How long it takes to write the article is dependent upon how much you already know about the topic and how quickly you can find the materials you need to research the topic. It is possible, working at a steady pace, to write ten 400-500 word articles in one day. That's $100 at $5 per article.

On the other hand, if you are a techie person and wish to do a steady business with your writing talent, you can create niche sites and place Google AdSense ads or promote affiliate products. In this way, you will not only make money from writing online, but also become able to setup a steady stream of automated income plan.

All you need to do is to target top paying niche, and write quality and informative articles on it and host it in your site. You will then start making money in an automated fashion.

There are sites that pay for content. Most of the sites require that you post your article first and wait for a buyer to come by to purchase your articles.

Associated Content buys the article from you. The pay is minimal from $3 to $5per 500 word article. However there are occasions where Associated Content has paid up to $50 per article. The articles can be submitted on an exclusive basis, meaning they aren't and won't be posted anywhere else, or nonexclusive, which means you, has used the article elsewhere.

It takes a day or two for Associated Content to review the article and make the offer. You are not required to accept the offer and can withdraw the article. It takes another two days for the article to be published and then two or three days for Associated Content to make the payment to you.

Websites That Pay For Articles

http://associatedcontent.com/

http://constant-content.com/

http://helium.com/

https://www.contentblvd.com/

http://www.articleteller.com/

http://digitaljournal.com/

https://www.triond.com/

http://www.fiverr.com/

http://experts.about.com/

http://blogging.org/

http://www.bukisa.com/

http://www.contentrow.com/

http://www.xomba.com/

http://wizzley.com/

It is a waste of money to help those who show no desire to help themselves.

Taylor Caldwell

Blogs That Pays For You To Writing

http://www.makealivingwriting.com/

http://beafreelanceblogger.com/

http://www.leavingworkbehind.com/

http://www.writersbucketlist.com/

http://www.writersincharge.com/

http://writetodone.com/

http://goinswriter.com/

http://thisisby.us/

http://bloggerparty.com/

http://www.5050articles.com/

http://www.journalhome.com/

http://www.softwarejudge.com/

http://www.fundsforwriters.com/

http://www.mindywrites.com/

Many people take no care of their money till they come nearly to the end of it, and others do just the same with their time.

Johann Wolfgang von Goethe

There are a number of sites you can post articles, tips, or essays to. You get paid a share of the earnings of the ads that show up with your article. The more popular your article, the more views, the more revenue you can earn.

Sites That Share Ad Revenue with Writers

http://www.best-reviewer.com/

http://www.flixya.com/

http://www.youtube.com/

http://www.bukisa.com/

http://www.infobarrel.com/

http://snipsly.com/

http://hubpages.com/

http://seekyt.com/

http://www.xomba.com/

A good reputation is more valuable than money.

Publilius Syrus

Pay Per Sale, Affiliate Programs, and Commissions

According to the highly respected Forrester Research, online affiliate marketing is expected to reach the all-time high of $230! This mammoth figure aptly describes one positive trend: that the entire affiliate marketing online is daily bulging at an alarming rate!

And if you remember the fact that affiliate merchants and affiliate marketers are the two credible forces driving these monumental figures, then you'll agree with me you should not fold your arms while the industry go burst with irregularities.

You're simply selling someone else's product through your marketing efforts, whether it's a blog or website, and you receive a sales commission when the sale is completed.

Most of these products are informational, an ecourse, software, or eBook. Quite a few of the affiliate products pay more than a 50% commission. The smart product owners offer banners, buttons, sales copy, and even articles that you can use to promote with.

- Clickbank is one of the most established programs.

- Commission Junction is another source. Both of these make the payments to the affiliates so you don't have to worry whether the product owner will pay.

- PayDotCom is a program which uses PayPal as the payment method. The product owner makes the decision to pay the affiliates and has to authorize PayDotCom to do so. Many products offer their own affiliate program independently. Look for one with a solid history of payment.

You can also become an affiliate of amazon.com to sell books and consumer products such as jewelry, televisions, whatever. The percentage commission is much lower, but sometimes the retail price is high enough to make up for it.

Here is an Affiliate Marketing Strategy Model. You can simply print out this page or save it on your desktop.

Step 1

Take Time (10-20 hours or even more) to choose a product to promote and write down a great, unique, and informative product   review. This is very important.

Step 2

Become an Affiliate of ClickBank, Amazon, or Commission Junction and generate an affiliate link for your product and put it on your review page and publish it on your website or a blog. Now, suppose if you are not the owner of any website or a blog then it's also perfectly alright. You can post your review on Squidoo, HubPages, WetPaints, and other sites of that nature.

Remember, all we need to do is publish your web page containing your affiliate link anywhere on the web and divert the web traffic towards it.

Step 3:

Link Building: This is very important. Your Affiliate link is live now. The only thing you have to do is drive web traffic towards it (the more the better). For this, you have to create and publish the content on other popular websites on the Internet and then put a link of your affiliate page.

Examples are EzineArticles, Squidoo, HubPages, WetPaint, YouTube, Xomba, eHow, WikiHow, Triond, Associated Content, Knol... etc...

Post content having your affiliate link page link on each of the above websites.

Step 4

Social Media: Try Facebook, Orkut, Twitter, Digg, Delicious, StumbleUpon & Reditt to divert more web traffic towards your affiliate links.

Step 5

Now sit back and wait for the web traffic to accelerate. This will probably take 1 week to 15 days to drive web traffic towards your affiliate page. Once the web traffic comes toward your page, you will definitely make money.

This is the Model of Affiliate Marketing Strategy. Nobody will teach you this.

Facebook Affiliate Marketing

How to Make Passive Income from Facebook Affiliate Marketing?

Affiliate marketing means selling other people's products from your web properties (Blogs & Websites) and getting commission for each sale you make. Many people have asked me: "How they can make money from Facebook Affiliate Marketing?"

Well, As far as I know, there is not any direct method of doing affiliate marketing on Facebook. But let's go to the basics and find out how we use Facebook to do affiliate marketing?

What is the Basic Principle behind Successful Affiliate Marketing?

Well, the basic principle of profitable affiliate marketing is - "The more web traffic you divert towards your Affiliate Links (Web pages having your affiliate links), the more Sales your affiliate links will generate."

This is the basic principle of Affiliate marketing and every theory and techniques of profitable affiliate marketing revolves around this simple basic principle.

Now, here we want to make money from Facebook affiliate marketing. So obviously, we need to find out the ways to divert traffic from Facebook to our affiliate links. Is this Possible? Well, Yes. There are several ways by which you can divert the web traffic on Facebook to your affiliate links.

Say for Example, Fan pages, Comments, News Feeds, Facebook applications, Direct Advertising on Facebook... etc...

By these methods, you can easily divert web traffic from Facebook to your own web property having affiliate links. The more web traffic that you divert to your affiliate links, the more sales it will generate and thus the more money you will make.

However, there is only one problem with Social Networking sites traffic and that is the traffic of social networking sites is not a buyer's traffic. They are there on the Social Network for being Social. So making money from Social Network traffic is really a difficult task.

Amazon

If you tell a person that it is possible to make money on Amazon easily they will commonly laugh your suggestion off, but the Amazon website really does make it simple for you to draw in some excellent profits with absolutely no difficulty. For a start, setting up an account is just a case of filling out a few online forms, and listing a product that already exists on the website is as complicated as completing all of around seven fields relating to condition and cost. It might sound like a cliche; to say, 'It's so simple a child could do it,' but when it comes to Amazon this is genuinely the case.

And if that wasn't enough, the sales giant has made things even easier with their new Fulfillment by Amazon service. Taking advantage of this option means that all you need to do is find your initial stock and send it to Amazon; they will literally take care of the rest!

The process is as simple as this:

1. You find the items that you want to sell on Amazon. You might have found them from a cheap wholesale supplier, or perhaps on another website such as eBay.

2. You send those items on to Amazon. It doesn't matter if the goods are brand new or have already been used as either condition can be sold on the website.

3. Amazon looks after all of your goods in their own warehouses. You guessed it; that means you don't even need to find space to store those boxes full of bits and pieces until they are sold.

4. You'll create your item listings on Amazon as if you yourself were handling the stock, but when someone orders one of your items it is Amazon that will actually handle the packaging and the shipping.

5. Your buyer receives what they ordered and you receive the cash (minus a handling charge that Amazon takes) - everybody wins!

It's true that the fees incurred by using the Amazon Fulfillment program are higher than those simply for selling through the website. However it's also true that costs for extra storage space, packaging materials and shipping costs could actually amount to more than this extra fee! And there's an added benefit; as you aren't really involved in the process of handling your goods, other than initially shipping them to Amazon, you can spend more of your important time researching other items to sell on for yet more profit!

I have no money, no resources, no hopes. I am the happiest man alive.

Henry Miller

MAKING MONEY FROM AMAZON

1. Sell Your E-Books on Amazon

- A lot of people think that they only sell physical products like books, electronic items, toys, fitness equipment and etc. It's true that most of the stuff available on Amazon are physical products. But you can also sell downloadable digital products such as your own e-books. So if you like writing and have wanted to be an author, you can actually start writing and publishing your own eBooks on Amazon.com.

EBooks are getting huge at the moment and with people being able to read their eBooks on gadgets like Kindle, iPhone and iPad, you can expect eBooks sales to soar higher and higher. If you enjoy writing and wanted to make some money, then this is something you might want to consider.

2. Amazon Affiliate Program

- Amazon has their own affiliate program which they called Amazon.com Associates. Their affiliate program has been around for a long time. And there are many people who made millions of dollars from their affiliate program. Basically what you can do is join their program and promote their products as an affiliate. You can just grab the affiliate banners and links and put them on your website. If your visitors happen to visit Amazon through your site and bought something, then you will be getting a commission for that. The commissions can sometimes be more than 4% of the product's price. So, let's say you're able to sell a $1000 HDTV; you'll be getting $40 commission. How cool is that?

BLOGGING

Money is always there but the pockets change; it is not in the same pockets after a change, and that is all there is to say about money.

Gertrude Stein

Years ago, blogging started out as a way for people to connect with each other sharing pictures, stories and experiences in their lives. Back then, it was thought of as more of an "online journal" of sorts; and in some instances today, it still is.

But over the years blogs evolved into marketing tools and became a way to make money both online and off.

If you've ever considered how to make money from blogging, here are a few ideas that may get you started in the right direction.

Income through AdSense Ads

Google offers a program called "AdSense" that lets online bloggers (and website owners) earn revenue from displaying advertisements on their site.

When you're accepted into the AdSense program, you can then place these ads on your own blog, and whenever one of your site visitors clicks on one of those ads you'll earn a certain amount of money.

The more clicks you receive, the more money you'll make. Now, the amount of money that Google will pay you differs greatly but usually ends up being a few cents per click. Although it doesn't sound like much at first, you can tell how this can add up to a great extent depending upon how many visitors your blog gets.

To generate income from adsense, you must create a lot of website. For example you create 20 website that generate $ USD 50 per month (per website). That extra $USD 300 per month. If you scale it to more than 300 website that more than $ 15000 per month. You cannot make a lot of money from one website. You must create an adsense empire network for your site. The more you built the website, you will earn more through adsense. This revenue will be generated and increase after month and years. This is the best passive income for you.

List of Adsense Alternative

Here, I provide you with the list of the alternative for adsense that can help you in making money from internet.

http://clicksor.com/

http://www.qadabra.com/

https://www.adversal.com/

http://chitika.com/

https://affiliate-program.amazon.com/

http://buysellads.com/

http://www.infolinks.com/

http://www.kontera.com/

Product Reviews

There are some websites online that connect you with other companies who need people to review their products. This helps to give the company more exposure and you can earn an income from it as well. Although often there are requirements for product reviews such as, the blog must have been around for some time and have a fair amount of visitors, you could still reap the benefits of doing product reviews if your site is accepted.

List of Product Review Site

http://www.consumersearch.com/

http://www.epinions.com/

http://sazze.com/index.html/

http://www.buzzillions.com/

http://www.dpreview.com/

http://www.crowdstorm.com/

Private Ad Sales

If your blog has been around for some time and you have decent traffic, you can advertise ad space for sale on your blog. The amount you'd charge for someone to advertise would be entirely up to you of course, but I would suggest taking a look at other blogs in your industry and see if they let people purchase advertising on their site. If they do, how much do they charge and for what size of an ad? This is yet another way to make money from your blog.

Affiliate Marketing

The term "affiliate marketing" encompasses a lot of areas I know. But just know that regardless of what kind of blog you run, and whatever it is you talk about, chances are there will be an affiliate program that you can join to help you earn money from your blog.

As an affiliate, you may want to consider Amazon.com program. Amazon especially can earn you a fair amount of money simply because there are so many options available that you could market. You could advertise books within your niche, software, games, clothing, electronics, and more. There really is no shortage of the amount of products that Amazon has that could help any blog owner earn some extra money here and there.

Where to Start?

You can start by signing up for a free Blogger account at Blogger.com. This is a popular free blogging service provided by Google that actually integrates AdSense ads **AND** Amazon advertisements. It will keep your expenses low and let you bring in that money that you're looking for while blogging about your interests.

Now that you have a blog, why don't you learn how to earn a residual income from your blog, it is not as hard as it sounds. Listed below are 3 of the best ways to start making money from your blog.

1. Sell advertising.

This is likely the most common means to generate income from your blog. If yours happens to become a well-known blog, or one that is well-received in a particular niche, it's always possible to sell ad space on your own. For lesser-known blogs, services such as Google's AdSense or BlogAds enable bloggers to establish ad programs.

Advertising can be broken into two section CPC (Cost per Click) and CPA (Cost per Action)

The top 3 CPC Networks are,

- AdSense: Google AdSense is probably the best known and most widely used way of making money from your blog.

- YPN People who have used YPN have said that they earn more per click when compared to AdSense revenue generated from the same site.

- Chitika. If you blog on a topic such as iPods, PSP, gaming, electrical accessories you will more than likely find Chitika generates a good revenue stream.

The top 2 CPA Networks are:

- AdBrite: If you have a high traffic blog and some room in your sidebar, then I would highly recommend signing up for AdBrite.

- Text-Link-Ads: You can apply to have your blog included in their marketplace so that advertisers can pay for their static text link on your site.

Here is the list TOP CPA network that you can join and start making money.

http://www.netpartner.com/

http://www.vcommission.com/

http://maxbounty.com/

http://affiliate.com/

http://shareasale.com/

http://www.cpaway.com/

http://www.convert2media.com/

http://www.clickbooth.com/

http://www.affiliateventuregroup.com/

http://adscendmedia.com/

http://yeahcpa.com/

http://www.cpalead.com/

https://peerfly.com/

http://www.adpushup.com/

http://www.leadbolt.com/

http://www.affiliatebot.com/

http://www.clixgalore.com/

http://alyads.com/

Do what you love and the money will follow.

Marsha Sinetar

2. Sell Products.

Affiliate programs enable your blog to serve as a conduit between readers and online sites offering various goods and services. One popular choice is Amazon.com. If, for instance, you offer book reviews or even just mention a book in passing in your blog, an affiliate program provides a means for your readers to click directly from your blog to Amazon to obtain further information about the book. If they break out the checkbook or charge card, you get paid as well, what a great way to make money from your blog.

- AzoogleAds If you have a blog about mobile phones, then you could offer a free ringtone download that would then pay out a few bucks once the customer downloads the ringtones. AzoogleAds have an excellent reputation in terms of their customer care and revenue share, you'll find that they pay out more than any other affiliate network. On the downside,

AzoogleAds do not have the widest range of offers, but if you are in the auto / finance / tech sector you'll be well catered for in making money from your blog.

- Commission Junction. These guys have been around for ages and have an absolutely gigantic number of affiliate programs to sign up to. If you have a blog that reviews products, chances are you will be able to find a suitable affiliate program in the CJ network and make money from your affiliate referrals. Your cut of each sale is not constant though, so make sure and check what % you get from each advertiser when you sign up with them.

3. Solicit contributions.

Not every blog-related income opportunity involves hawking goods or services. You could consider relying on the kindness of strangers to make money from your blog.

Ask for contributions, If for instance, your small-business blog supports a cause or issue in some fashion. Even if you've attracted a group of regular followers who simply enjoy reading what you have to say, they may be willing to underwrite their loyalty with a little financial help.

Programs such as PayPal make it easy to establish a simple on-site contribution collection button. Not the best way of generating revenue, but you can give it a try. PayPal is the best option of receiving funds. Or you could set up an Amazon gift list, this is another great way to make money from your blog.

EBAY

"While money can't buy happiness, it certainly lets you choose your own form of misery."

Groucho Marx

eBay is the premier online market place. Millions of eBay members bid for their favorite items on eBay every day. The draw of eBay is that it's a worldwide online auction center which exposes your merchandise to everyone, thus giving you an edge over selling your stuff to selected people in your local area. Selling on eBay is also not expensive as eBay charges a minimal amount per item auctioned.

More and more people on jumping on the eBay bandwagon and quitting their jobs to become sales entrepreneurs. One of the benefits of being a seller within the eBay community is having access to so many quality tools for support. One of those tools is eBay Pulse. For the seller who wants to make money on eBay this tool provides detailed information the most popular searches on eBay.

EBay Pulse can be found at eBay > Sell > Top Buyer Searches > eBay Pulse. Once at eBay Pulse, sellers will find a wealth of information that can help them make money on eBay. There are literally pages and pages of details about the most popular searches in almost all categories.

Do you know the top ten most popular searches on eBay? The top ten most popular eBay searches can be found on eBay Pulse. This information is based on the total number of searches and is important to those who want to make money on eBay.

The reason eBay has such mainstream success is actually because of its niche interests. EBay offers sellers the opportunity to instantly connect with millions of customers. It offers the opportunity for sellers and buyers of almost every type of merchandise to connect. Buyers can search eBay for deals on brand name clothing, hard to find collectibles, and rare antiques.

Inside eBay you will find categories, and subcategories, covering thousands of different products. A browser can easily spend countless hours searching eBay for unique items that match almost every type of interest, no matter how eclectic or obscure.

There are a lot more than 5 easy ways to make money from eBay and this will be a relatively short list. However, this list is great if you're just getting started or need to make some money fast!

1. The fastest and easiest way to make money on eBay is **to sell your unwanted gifts** and things that have been lying around the house for a while. This works particularly well if you're just getting started and you don't have that much experience with eBay selling. This is both fast and cheap since there's no real outlay on your behalf.

2. Visit car boot sales –

This is one of the most under-used tactics in the list. So many people don't really know the value of what they're selling. You can pick up lots of bargains using the buy cheap, sell high philosophy.

3. Visit charity shops –

One of my clients literally makes a living out of cheap Men's suits from these charity shops. I think it's because the perceived value is quite low but once listed on eBay with some nice pictures, a killer headline and description. You're able to ramp the price up and make a nice tidy profit. She makes a full time living by doing this on tip!

4. Sell information products –

This is my specialty and works really well. I happen to write and sell my own products by researching the topics from eBay pulse. EBay pulse basically allows you to find out what the most searched for items are in each category. I simply write a simple 15-20 page eBook that is in PDF format and then burn it to CD. The profit margins are high and the customer service is really low. My type of business.

5. Buy Retail, Sell Retail –

You're probably not aware of this, but most of the large stock websites actually get rid of excess stock on a regular basis. It's not good for them to hold onto inventory and they definitely don't want slow moving products on their shelves. I usually buy these products off their websites and then re-list them on eBay. There is a twist though...

Use Video To Increase Your Sales

I use small YouTube videos to increase my auction sales. I'm not just talking about me in front of a camera either. You can   put   PowerPoint   type presentation into your auctions to give the client more information and more interaction. You too can dominate markets and align yourself with other Powersellers on eBay.

List of Video Sharing Sites

https://www.netflix.com/

https://vimeo.com/

http://www.dailymotion.com/

http://www.hulu.com/

http://www.liveleak.com/

http://vube.com/

http://www.twitch.tv/

http://www.metacafe.com/

http://www.crackle.com/

http://www.viewster.com/

How to Make Money from eBay

The first task that a person needs to do is to choose a product they want to sell. The person must research what is selling that is available to you inexpensively. Remember that as a business person you must buy cheap and sell high. Pick an item that you are personally interested in and is unique.

Choose an item to sell that you are interested in as this will make it easier for you to find a bargain. After you have chosen a product then test the market. List a few of the items and see what happens. A great way to add value to your product is to find something that you can offer the product that no one else can offer. You will want to work on always selling the same type of product. You will want to understand the mindset of your customer and build your listings based on that mindset.

Building trust is vital to how to make money from eBay

Building trust is vital. Before you try to sell anything buy a few cheap items to build up your feedback on the site. Another great way to build up your trust level is to participate in forums related to your industry. People will then come to recognize and trust your name. Some of these forums will even let you post when you are featuring something on eBay.

Also make a website that links to your eBay store. The website shouldhave good search engine optimization. You can also do free article marketing which once again will help you develop your trust article. EBay also offers you the opportunity to become an expert on their site in a given niche and you should take advantage of this opportunity. Also make sure your customers get great customer service.

ADSENSE

"If you want to know what God thinks of money, just look at the people he gave it to."

Dorothy Parker

Want to know how to make money from AdSense? It's one of the easiest ways there are to make an income online. All you have to have is an ability to write and to understand keywords and niches. Let's talk about an easy way to make money from AdSense.

Google AdSense is the other side of AdWords. By that, I mean this. You know when you're on a blog or some other site and you see those Google ads? The advertisers who bought those ads actually only pay when someone clicks on the ad. That's called pay-per- click, or PPC marketing. When someone bids on a keyword phrase and writes an ad for their phrase, the ads can be put on sites like blogs and other content sites. When someone sees the ad and click, they go to the advertiser's site.

So, to learn how to make money from AdSense, you need to learn how to create a platform for content with these types of ads on it. People will read your content, then click on the ads.

That, fortunately, is not really that hard to do.

The first thing you need to do is to think of a topic to write about. In internet parlance, this is called a "niche". Once you get your niche, the next thing you have to know in order to learn how to make an income from AdSense is what phrases people are going to type into the search engines in order to find your site. These are called keyword phrases. There are number of free keyword search tools out there, one of the best is by Google. It's called Google External Keyword Tool.

Now that you know what to write about and what keyword phrases to stress, you'll need a platform to write on. Usually, that's a WordPress blog, although it could be something as easy as Blogger or Squidoo.

Finally, you just put this all together, text, platform, keyword phrases, and add in AdSense ads. As you get traffic, people will click on the ads and you'll make money! Yes, how to make money from AdSense really is that easy.

Even before you start with your website, you need to focus on the following 2 steps.

1. Keyword Research:

Once you have selected your topic for the site, it is important to do keyword research. Select keywords and phrases which people are searching for. For those relevant phrases or keywords, also check pages that will be competing with you. You may want to avoid highly competitive phrases as it will take much more effort for these phrases.

2. Write Articles:

Write original articles with keywords or phrases that you have shortlisted. If you decide to use PLR articles, then rewrite these articles in your own words. The articles that you write must be of quality and also relevant to the topic. Search engines reward quality content.

Aside from the focus on the keyword research and content article writing, the next focus is on the placement of the ads.

You will want to position ads where visitors to a site are most likely to click on them. For example, research shows that the top left has a high propensity for this.

The placement and tweaking of the colors and fonts of the ads are in themselves an art. So, if you think you are already making as much as you can make from your website, you might find that tweaking some of these ads may just increase the clicks.

Do Not Try To Trick Google

I have read of many schemes and hacks that you can do to make people come to your website and click on one of your AdSense blocks. The people who try to trick Google in this way are not successful and do not make money. They might say they are making money but they are lying to you. Google has really got its act in order and you can rest assured that if you try to trick Google you will fail.

How To Make A Website for Google AdSense

You should look on the AdSense model as a way of monetizing your website. What you should not do is make a website purely with the aim of trying to make an AdSense income. These things are not the same. Your website should be full of words, videos, links and other content that attracts lots of visitors. It should be tightly themed on one topic and be regularly updated with new pages and information. The AdSense part of your website will be one of the options for your visitor to take when they visit your website. If this sounds like too much work then this type of internet marketing is not for you.

- **The Tighter the Niche the Better.**

I have one website that is full of information on a tiny niche in the health foods area. There are tiny amounts of searches for this topic but likewise there is little competition. This website outperforms all my other websites put together in terms of AdSense income because it is so full of great content and relevant information. My diet website has many more pages and receives hundreds of daily visitors and yet doesn't come close to my health niche site.

- **Write For Your Human Visitors**

It never fails to astound me when so called experts say you should write with the search engines in mind. This is simply rubbish. Write for your true visitors and if they like what they read and see they will stay around longer. If you have had to work at making your content search engine friendly it can come over a stilted and messy. As a writer you should picture your reader as an individual sitting opposite you. How would you say your piece to them? That is how you should write.

Although people provide some guidance, ultimately it is your own experimenting that will show you what gives you the best returns.

When you make money from AdSense and want to increase this, an additional tool that you have from AdSense is the excellent tracking statistics. You should make use of this to see which are driving the money making clicks and which are not. This gives tremendous information to decide how to fine tune to your ads.

Make it a point to keep a journal of the changes you make and the results you are getting. You can then apply your own learnings to make money from AdSense.

You need time, dedication and patience to make this work and to get the money rolling in. You cannot set up a site and expect the clicks to happen. You still need to do some maintenance to keep the site going, but not as intensive as when you first started.

While these are the concepts, it is best to get access to resources that will provide you detailed guidance to help you with the actual work.

CONCLUSION

Anybody who thinks money will
make you happy hasn't got money.

David Geffen

I hope that you will get benefit when reading this eBook and gain knowledge from the technique that has been shared here. All the techniques underlying in this eBook can be used as the guidelines to help you start your business online.

Feel free to email me if you need answer to start your first internet business. I will be glad to help you on your first journey making money online.

All the BEST

W M HIRWANI W HUSSAIN

wmhwh12@gmail.com

www.ingramcontent.com/pod-product-compliance
Lightning Source LLC
Chambersburg PA
CBHW051816170526
45167CB00005B/2034